The REAL Joy of SAILING

C.S. Henry

Inquiries should be addressed to:

Creighton S. Henry
Creighton Hall Publishing
36 Wright Avenue
Toronto, Ontario M6R 1K8

Printed in Canada by
Promark Printing Inc.
1995

ISBN 0-9697745-0-8

Acknowledgements

To the many kind and helpful sailors we met along the way. With special thanks to:

Jim and Judy (Aquilo), who towed us so much our bow stretched six inches.

Vince and Jane (Anhram), who gave new meaning to the expression "are we having fun yet?"

Joe and Dorothy (Valkyrie), who showed me how to tighten the packing gland on a sinking boat.

Al and Marilyn (Temptress), who through ingenious techniques showed us how to stow a ton of provisions aboard a 5-ton boat in preparation for the Bahamas.

Greg and Linda and Megan and Colin (Southern Trails), who made us aware of the importance of replacing precious bodily fluids on a regular basis and the nutritional value of Dockside Cheeseburgers with the works.

Bob and Ulla (Apawawahka), whose cool heads and quick action prevented mass hysteria aboard Fidelio II when the shaft and prop fell out, and the warm waters of Marsh Harbour poured in.

And to all our friends and fellow sailors at the Port of Newcastle Marina.

Dedication

This book is dedicated to Karen ... my first mate, my friend, my inspiration ... and my typist.

Karen ... are you sure we can't settle this out of court?

Foreword

The author, having arranged a one year sabbatical from unemployment, purchased and then sailed a 29-foot Alberg sailboat, Fidelio II from Newcastle on Lake Ontario to the Abaco Islands in the Bahamas.

He shares with you the thrill of turning "the dream" into reality and hopes that many of the observations and tips found throughout this book will add to your sailing pleasure and give you a deeper insight into the "Real Joy of Sailing".

A network of rivers, lakes and canals, all leading to the sea, await the cruising sailor. Strange new countries and distant ports are calling, and who knows, with a fair wind and a lot of luck, he might even arrive at the right one.

How Big and How Much

Two questions the prospective sailor asks are: (1) what size boat should he consider and (2) how much will he have to spend? The answer to both these questions is found in the rule: "You can only sail a boat as large as the loan you can float." Therefore, the next step is to find who you can put the arm on, for how much, and where they can be found. No problem! See your friendly bank manager, the man who understands. Make an appointment to crawl in and discuss your plans. Be prepared to spend at least a half hour listening to a tirade of abuse, ridicule and sarcasm, but in the end, driven by greed, and a high interest loan, he will tell you just how much you're good for and with that information, you'll know whether to look for a 12-footer or a 12-meter.

"YOU want ME to lend you money for a BOAT?

If after cleaning out the savings account and the kids' piggy bank, you're still a little short, don't worry. There are other ways of raising extra cash. Have a yard sale. Sell the furniture. Sell all the kids' toys. Sell the kids. If you're still short, why not increase the mortgage, sell the second car, sell the first car? How about cashing in the family insurance or your pension plan? You know how much pet food costs these days. How about old Rover? Turn those liabilities into instant money.

Having thought over everything carefully (ruling out the safer forms of recreational travel such at hang-gliding,white water rafting or mountain climbing) a quick trip to a marine psychiatrist may be in order. This new, rapidly expanding branch of medical specialists is listed in the yellow pages of most phone books under "Marine Services".

Your compass may be off a few degrees.

Shopping Around

There are many ways to look for a boat. Some of them are: attending boat shows, scouring the classifieds, talking to brokers. You might also like to try, in addition to these time-proven methods, other approaches that often yield excellent results. They are:

1. Searching Boatyards - The best time is in the dead of winter when prices are at their lowest. Besides, what's more enjoyable than struggling through snow up to your holding tank, in the bitter cold, or clawing your way up an ice-laden steel cradle to read an unreadable phone number on the "for sale" sign. If you are stout-hearted enough and survive ... you may find the boat you're looking for!!

Note: Review your life insurance policy carefully before using this method. You may not have adequate coverage. Would-be buyers are found in boatyards every spring ... just under the melting snow.

The dead of winter is the best time to search the boat yards.

2. Buy a Greek fisherman's cap and hang around

marine parking lots. Keep your eyes and ears open. Vigilance is often well rewarded. Spotting the pale faced captain, who's supposed to be at work, trying to explain to his wife, who's sitting behind the wheel of a "Rented Wreck", just what he's doing with the office nymphomaniac on board, could mean there will be a boat up for grabs the next day. Cheap!

Sometimes information of this nature comes along and can be turned into a bit of hard cash. This is tacky but, you want a boat, don't you?

3. Watch the obituaries: Considered to be the last straw

in tastelessness, the results are often most rewarding. With a little digging, it's amazing what one can turn up. A simple phone call to the bereaved, posing the question, "Is your boat for sale?", will get one of three responses: i) "No ... He didn't even own a boat." ii) "Why ... Uh ... Yes, let's talk." or, iii) "You — creep, how could you ask at a time like this?" You now know that numbers (ii) and (iii) do have boats. A few more discrete questions and if it sounds good and it's a pleasant day, why not attend the service? A few words of sympathy and who knows ... many a good deal has been nailed down this way ... ask any funeral director!

Remember. Whatever method you use, be persistent.
Somewhere out there a boat is waiting with yours
and the bank manager's name on it.

Tips When Buying

The descriptive phrases often used by the sellers of boats would warm the heart of a used car salesman. An understanding of some of these terms can be of great help in determining the condition of the boat.

What the seller says	What the seller means
It's a really fine boat.	It's slowly falling apart.
They don't build them like this any more.	After the first five sank, the government stopped them. This is the sixth.
I'm looking for something a little bigger.	I'm buying a 36-foot motor home.
I haven't got time to look after it.	It's falling apart faster than I can fix it.
The wife isn't too fond of sailing.	She's been gone for five years.
She's cozy.	Great for two people 4 ft. 3 in. or less.
Good in heavy weather.	Needs a gale to get her moving.

A little cosmetic work and you'll be out sailing in no time.

Should you find a boat that interests you, be sure to check out the following

- If it is a cabin model, can you stand comfortably or are you prepared to spend every other week at the chiropractor's?

- Are the companionway and hatches large enough to pass through easily?

- How about guests? Would they be comfortable? When the claim is to sleep six people is that side by side or double-stacked?

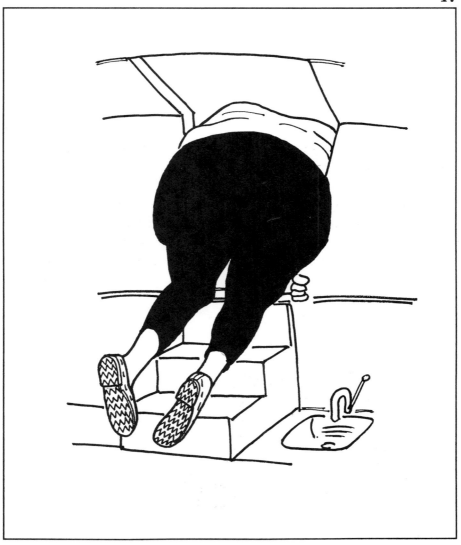

This is not a pretty sight.

Is the head easy to get into? How big is it? Most important of all, can you turn around in it?

Can two people move about comfortably above and below decks? This is determined largely by the beam (width). Boats of identical length can vary greatly in beam. Beam has been used to describe "width" for generations. e.g. "Boy ... is she broad in the beam" or "She's two axe handles across the beam", a phrase well know to every farm boy.

You've Found It

Congratulations! You have found the boat, taken the plunge and are now the proud owner of a magnificent sailing yacht. There she sits, your dream come true, bobbing saucily at dockside waiting just for you. If this is the first time you've seen her in the water, do try to control yourself. Hollering, jumping or running around in a frenzy are strictly out. Sailors are always cool.

Dress properly. Show up unshaven. Wear an old pair of cords, a moth- eaten turtleneck and a pair of worn docksiders, sans socks. Keep your hands shoved down into the rear pockets. Chew on an old pipe, then when you reach your newly acquired liability, stop and eye-ball her slowly from bow to stern. Look up and down the mast. Frown slightly as if you have spotted something. Look wise, squint your eyes. Mutter a little bit to yourself. This will help to give the impression that you really are an "old salt" and actually know what you are doing. It also gives you time to find out how to climb on board.

It has happened that new owners, in a state of near hysteria, have, after running along the dock screaming their heads off, leaped wildly on board only to find out that they are on the wrong boat. This can be not only embarrassing, but downright dangerous, especially if the owner happens to be aboard too.

Boarding Her

A note of caution for the first-time sailor. The moment you step on board ready to "take her out", everything you have learned from books, instruction manuals, and videotapes will disappear completely from your mind. At the shouted words "Shall we cast off your line, Skipper?", the brain numbs and the eyes glaze over, vision blurs.

The only known antidote for this condition is one-half a tumbler of navy rum followed by a full tumbler of navy rum, and it must be administered immediately.

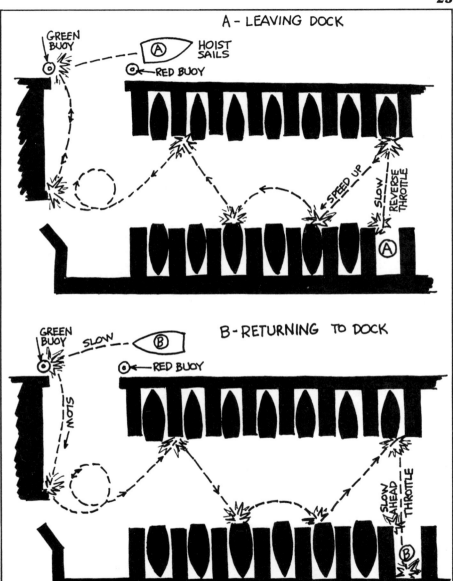

Be careful when leaving or returning to the docks. Boat owners are touchy about being hit, and retribution can be swift!

Taking Her Out

When you first venture away from the dock it is advisable to have someone extra as crew. This can be either a person with many years of experience who will do everything correctly while you stand at the wheel and look good, or, one who has never been on a boat, does everything wrong, while you stand at the wheel still looking good.

Should your wife be crewing, it is strongly recommended that all sharp instruments (knives, scissors, etc.) be locked up with two different padlocks, each spouse having only one key. This is for the protection of both parties.

Until the captain and crew gain experience working together, it is suggested that the vessel leave the dock under engine power only, striking as few other boats as possible, rather than attempting to "sail off". When you are well away from land and the sounds of the outraged skippers whose boats you have just side-swiped, then is the time to hoist sail ... quickly.

Sailing (basic)

1. First, haul up the main sail and secure the halyard.

2. Next, haul up the jib and secure the jib halyard.

3. Secure the main sheet.

4. Secure the jib sheet.

If the boat moves, you are sailing. If you are sailing, you are a sailor. Steering, heading up, sheeting in, coming about, letting out, etc. – all of these skills are nothing more than simple refinements of the basics, and are easily mastered over a 10 to 15 year period.

Within 20 minutes of getting underway, chances are one of two things will happen. The wind will either die completely, or develop into a full gale. If it dies and you wish to return to the marina, simply start the engine, point the sharp end of the boat toward the dock and head in. If it blows into an 80 mph gale, have your camcorder handy as there is bound to be plenty of action and excitement ... real excitement!

Great Frieda ... now this time I'll attach it to the sail.

Knots

As a sailor, you should know about knots. Knots are what keep your boat secure ... knots keep your boat from sloshing about the marina and driving her bowsprit through your neighbour's hull. Knots are what happens to your stomach when you think about casting off. Learning to tie a knot quickly could save your life. The sample shown in fig. 1 is the Common Knot and by far the most popular. It has many uses.

Parts of a rope:

① END   ② IN BETWEEN   ③ OTHER END

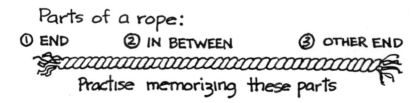

Practise memorizing these parts

Common Knot
FIGURE 1

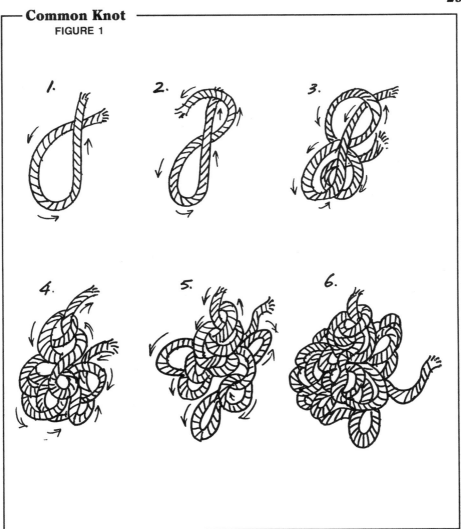

Sailors should know their knots and be able to tie them quickly.
The Common Knot as shown in fig. 1, is by far the most popular.
Learn to tie it using one hand only.

Fig. 2

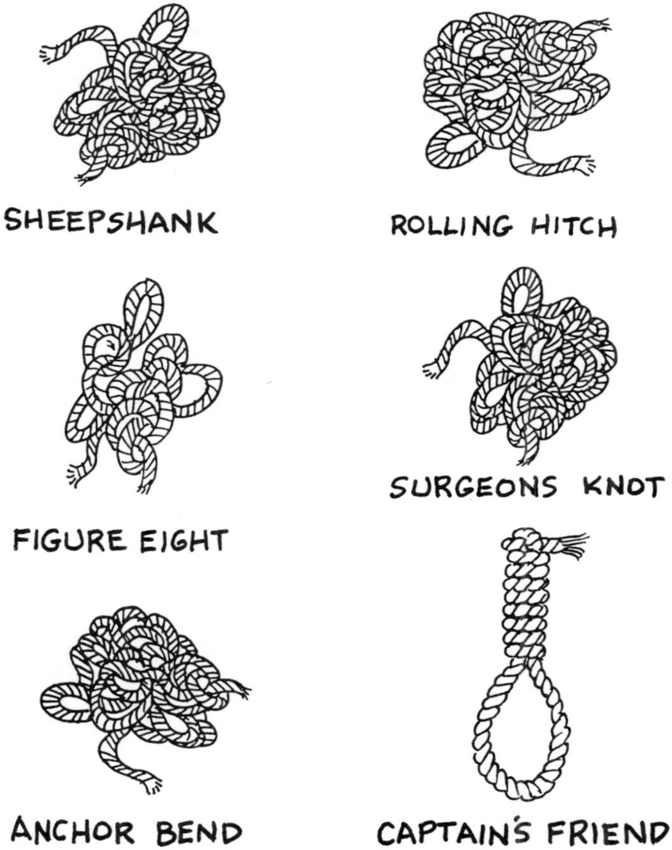

SHEEPSHANK

ROLLING HITCH

FIGURE EIGHT

SURGEONS KNOT

ANCHOR BEND

CAPTAIN'S FRIEND

Other popular knots

Cruising

Recommended Study Courses

Marine Engines: Gas or Diesel
1. How to disassemble, re-assemble, disassemble, re-assemble.

*2. Making the Most of Carpenters' Tools (For Beginners) - what you need ... their uses ... keeping them sharp.

*3. First Aid — How to Stop Massive Bleeding, Stitching Made Easy, and Simple Treatment for Shock. (It is recommended that courses 2 and 3 be taken together.)

4. Plumbing and Head Problems (Theory) — Identifying Them by Nose ... How to Correct Them ... Simple Treatment for Chronic Nausea.

5. Practical Electricity — Battery Care ... Fuse Testing and the Safe Way to Administer Shock Treatment as a Means of Relieving Stress.

6. Coastal Navigation — With the Use of Road Maps.

Suggested Supplementary Reading

1. Self Help Through Hypnosis

2. An Introduction to Modern Psychiatry

3. Saving Your Marriage Without a Counsellor

4. Saving Your Marriage With a Counsellor

5. The Power of Prayer

Canals and Locks

A lock is simply an enclosed chamber (generally a part of a canal system) that, when entered, is designed to move your craft (1) up (2) down or (3) sideways. The sideways position in conjunction with either of the first two will depend upon how well your boat has been secured. Water simply rages in, raising the boat, or it rages out, lowering it. There is nothing to fear but fear itself.

As there is a lot of motion caused by turbulence, the boat must be kept slightly away from the wall at all times to prevent the tearing apart of the hull. Teamwork is essential here. Although there has never been a boat lost during this operation, many a good marriage has wound up on the rocks.

Lockmasters are always cheerful and have a delightful sense of humour.

That was great, now shall we try it one more time?

No No No. I want it on THAT one OVER THERE.

No Harry, I don't know where the brown handled knife is.

Why, oh why, do they do it to themselves.

Officials have reported seeing 90 pound wives taking on 200 pound husbands ... and winning! On one occasion, a lockmaster had to use a crow bar to force apart the fingers of a woman's hands that were firmly wrapped around her husband's throat. Marriages should be on a solid foundation before entering the locks.

Some sailors actually claim to enjoy going through the locks. Avoid them! They might be dangerous.

After the locks ... sharing a few quiet moments together.

Sail has right-of-way over power.
If you believe that, you probably believe in the tooth fairy.

Preparation for Overhead Bridges

It is often necessary, prior to entering a canal, in order to avoid collision with overhead bridges, to un-step (take down) the mast. The lowered mast is secured lengthwise to either the starboard or port deck in exactly the correct position to ensure breaking the ankle, tearing the achilles tendon, separating the cartilage from the kneecap ... or all three.

Another ideal place to store the mast is dead amidship over the companionway where one's skull, upon upward contact, drives the head downward into the chest cavity, or, if going below, one's chin, upon contact, smartly snaps the head back, positioning, for an instant, the base of the skull between the shoulder blades.

You just broke last week's record Fred!

Secure the mast on either the port side or starboard deck.

Anchoring

Anchoring or "dropping the hook", as seasoned sailors say, has two purposes: to hold the vessel more or less in the same place, and to provide free entertainment for those already at anchor. The routine is fairly predictable, especially if the helmsman and crew are married. As the vessel nears the desired spot, the crew at the bow, with anchor ready (1) gives a secret hand signal to the helmsman, (2) then, the helmsman mumbles instructions to the crew, (3) the crew glares at the helmsman, (4) the helmsman hisses at the crew, (5) the crew snarls at the helmsman, (6) helmsman rushes toward crew, cursing, (7) crew drops anchor on helmsman's foot, then helmsman, white-faced with pain, lifts anchor from flattened foot and drops it over the side. (8) Crew wins!!

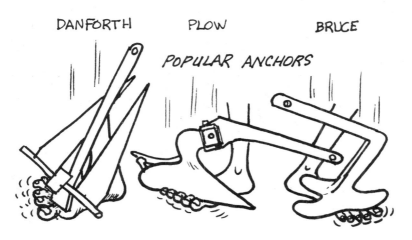

DANFORTH   PLOW   BRUCE

POPULAR ANCHORS

Anchoring · Practical Hand Signals

1. *Reduce Speed*
2. *Starboard a little*
   (to port if arm in
   other direction.)
3. *Increase speed*

4. *Hold Steady*
5. *Try again.*
6 & 7. *The same to*
   you too!

An **anchor** is said to be **dragging** when a vessel moves in reverse to a new location. That might be the hull of another boat, the pier or even the breakwall, depending on the direction of the wind and current.

An **anchor** is said to be **in drag** when it is on board and decorated with bits and pieces of female clothing.

Anchoring is a skill that develops quickly and with a lot of practice can often be **mastered within 5 years**.

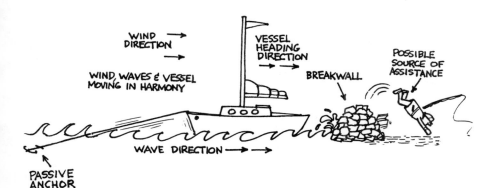

Will you look at that. They're all dragging their anchors except us.

Weighing Anchor

Now ·w·w·w· you're getting it.

The Joys of "Overnighting"

Spending the night at anchor as opposed to tying up to a dock is the way seasoned salts prefer to cruise. It's cheaper and far more exciting.

The first couple of nights' sleep may be difficult as one feels the arthritis starting to take hold beneath the damp sheets. The sounds that one thought were caused by a mild internal problem, brought on by a tinned tuna and beans dinner, may be the rumbling of distant thunder.

As the wind picks up outside (or is it inside?), a halyard may gently slap the mast. Out of bed, up on deck, and tie off the offending line only to return to bed and hear two more different sounds, it's back on deck, find the culprit, secure it and then return below.

This little operation, along with checking the anchor, may be repeated every 15 minutes or so and usually allows for a total night's sleep of about half an hour.

The sounds of silence.

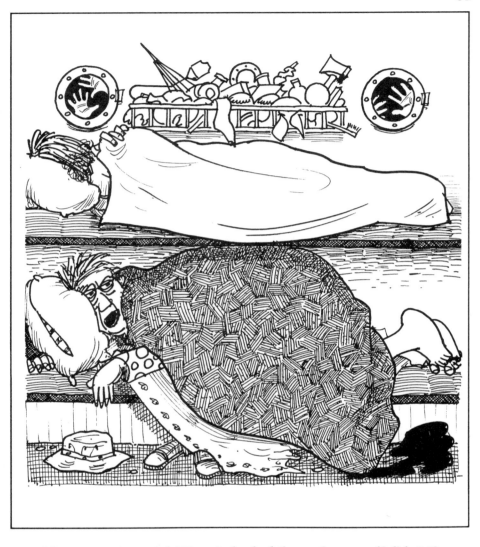

Of course we're not drifting. I checked the anchor myself didn't I?

Do not leave hatches open at night in a tight anchorage.

Social Life

The cocktail hour is a ritual among cruising sailors and eagerly anticipated after an exhilarating day of sailing. Should you find yourself in a position of being "host", knowing what to offer your guests in the way of refreshments is important, but not difficult. Put simply ... if it can be poured ... they will drink it. The cocktail hour usually starts around fiveish and ends around elevenish.

In the evening, everyone loves to get together just to chat or swap yarns. Being, for the most part, free spirits, little interest is taken in the "outside world". "It's the same old story anyway," they all agree. "Who wants to hear about the amount of crime in the streets, the corruption, and the misery? Not us!", they say. "Let's keep things light and simple."

As the evening progresses, wonderful sea stories may be told about hurricanes, ships striking rocks, dismastings, family boats sinking, and entire families disappearing at sea.

This light hearted humour may continue on until the wee hours of the morning.

He's from that 22 footer over there sir and would like to invite you and the ladies aboard for cocktails; however as it could be a little crowded, he'll be happy to join you here.

After an evening of socializing,
make sure you board the right boat ... yours.

Rafting Up

Rafting Up is an anchoring technique that is often used where space is limited, or, more likely, a number of sailors simply want to get together and do a little visiting.

One boat sets an anchor, usually the largest one, and the others simply tie up to it on either side. When completed, the whole thing resembles a raft. A very large raft.

This is a cozy arrangement and allows the crew members to move freely from one vessel to another.

A true test of seamanship comes into play when, after five or six hours of socializing the crew try to find the way back to their own boat; without getting their hands stepped on . . . Some never make it.

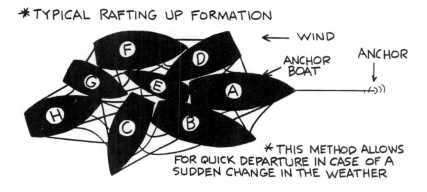

*TYPICAL RAFTING UP FORMATION

← WIND

ANCHOR BOAT

ANCHOR

* THIS METHOD ALLOWS FOR QUICK DEPARTURE IN CASE OF A SUDDEN CHANGE IN THE WEATHER

Rafting up with other boats is such fun isn't it Freddie?

The Weather

Marine weather forecasts are basically broken down into three parts with varying degrees of accuracy. First, what the weather did yesterday, accurate to 100%, what it's doing right now, accurate about 60% and what it's going to be doing tomorrow, given in possible percentages of probabilities and accurate about 2% of the time.

Heavy Weather

Heavy weather is sailor-talk for wind and waves. BIG WIND and BIG WAVES.

MARINE WEATHER FORECASTING EQUIPMENT

Forecasts

And now for your local marine forecast but frankly folks
it looks so bad I don't have the heart to read it to you.

Seasickness

If a member of the crew or a guest should become seasick, simply ask him to move to the opposite end of the boat. If he insists on being close to you, then it is advisable to put on a wet suit and position the victim downwind.

Should he feel more comfortable hanging over the side, then make certain to lash his ankles firmly to the deck.

The use of a portable radio headset is a great way to block out the gagging, retching, gargling sounds produced by the afflicted person.

HEAVY WEATHER KIT

Always be sure to have foul weather gear and plenty of food on board in case you get "caught out" in heavy weather. Keeping warm, dry and well- nourished is all part of the Joy of Sailing and essential for ones comfort, safety and sanity.

Bon appétit.

Every vessel should maintain a well stocked first aid cabinet in case of accident. Many excellent non-prescription medicines are available at drug stores, grocery stores and package stores. Seafaring people have used these medications for decades with great success. However, you must be 21 years of age and be able to prove it before injuring yourself.

Problem	Medication	Dosage
Minor cuts, scrapes and burns	Gimlet 3/4 oz. gin 1/4 oz. triple sec 2 oz. lime juice Shake ingredients with ice & strain. Garnish: Cherry	Before dinner Before retiring
Minor breaks, dislocated shoulder, hip or lower back.	Side Car 3/4 oz. brandy 1/4 oz. cointreau 2 oz. lemon juice Combine ingredients with ice cubes and shake. Strain into cocktail glass.	Before meals Between meals Between meals After meals
Ripped cartilage, torn tendons, severe sprains.	Rusty Nail 3/4 oz. Scotch 1/4 oz. Drambuie Pour ingredients over ice cubes. Garnish: cherry.	Whenever requested
Sunburn, sunstroke hypothermia	B-52 1/3 oz. Kahlua 1/3 oz. Baileys 1/3 oz. Grand Marnier	Whenever victim regains consciousness.
Complete mental and emotional breakdown.	Velvet Hammer 1/2 oz. Cointreau 1/4 oz. White Creme de Cacao 1/4 oz. Kahlua 2 oz. cream Blend ingredients with Ice cubes and shake. Strain into mug.	As required

Here's some soup dear but be careful, it's scalding hot.

"What are you taking all those clothes for?" you said.
"It's warm where we're going." you said.
Charlie, you're an absolute scream.

Marinas

Wherever boats sail, you'll find marinas nearby, offering fuel, docking facilities, laundry, showers etc.

Many marinas are "full service" and have towing and repair facilities available. Because of their natural love of the sea and sailors in particular, their charges are often embarrassingly low.

They are usually located between two and 10 miles from the spot where you break down.

Docking charges are based on the overall length of the vessel from stem to stern.

Showers are usually available, for a fee. If however you're tight with a buck, wait for a day or two and when the wind shifts, one of the neighbours will probably offer to <u>treat</u> you and your crew to a shower.

All marinas appreciate sailors! This is because they are known as "BIG SPENDERS". Marinas love being presented with credit cards for four dollars' worth of gas. Rolling their eyes and sighing is the traditional way of saying "thanks".

No, No, No, let me guess.
You want three dollars worth of gas, do I have any water, is there a place
to dump garbage, can you tie up for an hour or so,
and do I have a phone you can use.

Simple solution to saving money.

Who's gonna find out. What can they do to you? Throw you in jail?
No way I'm paying two bucks for a lousy shower.

Shopping

Shopping, disposing of garbage, getting ice, doing laundry etc., are tasks that are traditionally the responsibility of the crew and as such are jealously guarded. With the development of sturdy fold-up shopping carts and tough nylon back packs, bigger loads reduce the number of trips allowing more time for the crew to prepare meals and scrub decks.

Average size load of provisions for 2 people for 2 weeks.

Modern Shopping Malls and Bargain Centers are often located near popular anchorages. Many offer BIG SPECIALS to the sailing community with up to 25% or more, added to the regular price.

When shopping for supplies most crew use the old rule of thumb "buy three of everything". Hey . . . you never know.

Get out the dinghy Cap'n.
I can smell a shopping mall out there somewhere.

I said, while the clothes are drying how about picking up a case of twenty-four and a bag of ice and <u>then</u> go back and get the groceries.

The town laundromat is a wonderful way to meet the friendly locals.

Sightseeing

After a week or two on board you may suffer from a bout of "cabin fever". If you do, then make a change and head for shore.

Hiking through the streets and laneways of the many quaint, colorful little towns that are found along the waterways is a great way to stretch the old legs and bone up on local history.

Villagers are always helpful and ready to point the way to any of the friendly merchants in town or, if you want, they will even walk you personally to the store where a smiling merchant will separate you from your cash faster than you can say "haul up the anchor".

*They weren't as expensive as the other kind
and the salesman said they're just as good
and coast guard approved too.*

I used to be a mechanic but after a couple of years of retirement,
I had to have something to do and this seemed so natural.

You're in luck sir, here comes our mechanic now.

Engines

Today's marine engines, while being very dependable (sometimes running for two days in a row), require occasional maintenance. To make this pleasant task even more enjoyable, make sure that you have only standard-sized wrenches for a metric engine, and metric sized wrenches for a standard engine. The fun of trying to tighten a critical 7/16 inch engine nut, with a 12 mm wrench while drifting toward a breakwall is something not to be missed.

Often a crew member will station him/herself nearby offering words of encouragement like, "Why are you doing that?", "Why don't we call in a REAL mechanic?", "Why?", etc. This kind of assistance is a great help, as it speeds up the work pace, thus getting you on your way that much sooner.

Repairing engines is a happy learning experience.

Hubert has eight hundred and seventy three wrenches.
But does he have the right one? You guessed it

SEE? IT SAYS RIGHT HERE IF THE RED LIGHT COMES ON STOP ENGINE AND CONTACT NEAREST DEALER IMMEDIATELY
WELL GEE WHIZ BARBARA THAT SURE MAKES THE WHOLE THING A LOT EASIER

Navigation

na´ vig/ate — to set a course (more or less) to weave, stagger, crawl from point A — (dockside bar) to point B (dinghy, vessel or waiting squad car); ~ to assist skipper by indicating proper route of passage by gesturing, pointing and cursing.

na´ vig/a/tor – The navigator (the one who has the charts) can be very secretive at times, not allowing the helmsman (the one who steers) to <u>see</u> the charts, but instead, demanding to accept without question, that they are where they're supposed to be. This does not always work.

Running Aground

.. it happens

If while underway, your vessel should come to a sudden stop, you've probably run aground, or, as the old salts say "run out of water". These things happen and when they do, it's important to keep calm and not panic. The sickening WHUMP that is heard may be no more than the keel separating from the hull, or some other minor problem.

It often happens, at times like this, that the tide is actually rising, in which case you should float free in a short while; however, should it be ebbing, it might take a few hours . . . quite a few hours . . . but you will get off . . . eventually.

If you decide to "wait it out" then make good use of the time and have an in-depth discussion of the grounding. Carefully assess the situation, find out what went wrong and why, and then (here is the really good part), whose fault it was.

Not only are "grounding discussions" informative but they offer a great opportunity for the captain and crew to really get to know each other on a whole new level.

A phenomenon of these discussions is that the volume and number of colourful words used always rises as the tide lowers, and lowers as the tide rises. Look at it all as a new learning experience.

A tow might work, but be certain you're not too hard aground. Nothing will remove a piece of the forward deck, pulpit or part of the hull faster than an overly zealous yachtsman on a 40 footer sporting twin 600 h.p. diesels "rescuing" a sailboat.

It says ... You have gone aground at high water ... have a nice day.

Kedging Off

Should you go aground through a navigational error, and there is no one close by to assist, you might try to kedge yourself off. As disgusting as this may sound it is a technique that is guaranteed to get some kind of result. Simply take an anchor (by dinghy, if you have one) to a depth of water required to float your boat and set it. Then, with the rope around a winch, crank in. This will either move the vessel to deeper water, pull the anchor out altogether, or give you a football-sized hernia.

Or, if you choose, you can always try reverse throttle and running astern (Backing off). If you do, one of four things will probably happen:

1. You'll suck so much bottom sand into the cooling system the engine will be hot for a month.

2. The transmission will self-destruct.

3. The reverse thrust will cause the shaft to unscrew and fall out.

4. All of the above will happen.

Kedging off

Now throw it out there as far as you can.

Pets

Many sailors like having their pets on board. Cats and dogs in particular are very popular. If you are taking the family pooch aboard for the first time, then it should be on a leash and secured to the mast. This will stop them from repeatedly throwing themselves overboard and heading for the safety of shore.

If Fido insists on doing this, then attach a long bungee cord instead of a leash. Then, the further out the he leaps, the faster he'll return to the deck - and usually dry!

For the weekend sailor there is the weekend pet, a great source of fun and companionship. These splendid little creatures, although independent by nature, always come when they are called and are very easy to care for.

Requiring little more that a good Beaujolais or Bordeaux (lightly chilled) and soft music, their warm and affectionate nature provides great comfort to the lonely sailor tied to the dock night after night.

When the time comes for them to leave, these delightful pets, not wishing to disturb anyone, always disembark soundlessly in the dark, usually alone, and head straight for the parking lot where, as amazing as it may seem, most of them have cars parked. Their own cars ... big cars.

Weekend species

I don't understand it.
She's supposed to be visiting her mother in Arizona this weekend.

Insects

Flying, creeping or crawling insects, while a nuisance, are generally harmless enough. These minor annoyances can be reduced substantially through the liberal use of insect repellants. Your crew will probably be reduced substantially too ... but, what the heck ... it smells nice, doesn't it?

Remember ... don't fire until you can see the reds of their eyes.

Hurry Martha hurry. If they get him, who will be next.

AIR HORN?
I thought it was a can of insect repellant.

Plumbing

Recommended Reading:

The voluminous study "The Theory of Modern Marine Plumbing" by Schoenhiser (32,000 pages) is still to this day, considered to be the most comprehensive and thoroughly researched work of this century.

Over the years his theory has often been attacked by so-called "modernist movements" but, in the end, the work prevails. Seeking to resolve the question "Why are there no minor problems ... only major ones, Schoenhiser set out looking for the answer in 1912 and continued research until 1936, at which time his findings were published. He died on his yacht "Genevieve" in 1938 while attempting to unplug the head with a coat hanger. One of the crew noticed the head door was open and he closed it. Schoenhiser, who was on his hands and knees at the time, was suddenly thrown forward striking the inside of the bowl with his head. As near as can be determined, his right knee came up, forcing the hand valve to the flush position, and at the same time, opening the sea cock. It was duly noted on the certificate as "Death by Drowning".

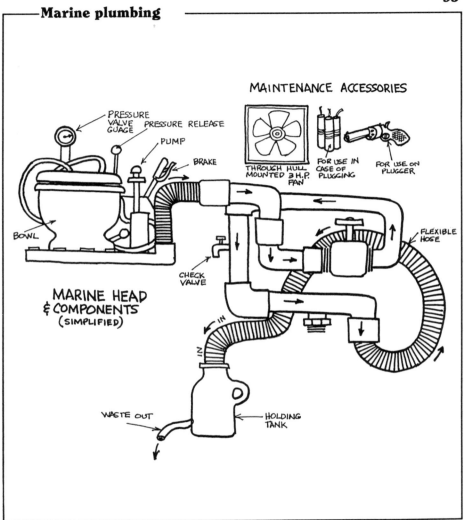

MAINTENANCE ACCESSORIES

THROUGH HULL
MOUNTED 3 H.P.
FAN

FOR USE IN
CASE OF
PLUGGING

FOR USE ON
PLUGGER

PRESSURE
VALVE
GUAGE

PRESSURE RELEASE

PUMP

BRAKE

BOWL

FLEXIBLE
HOSE

CHECK
VALVE

MARINE HEAD
& COMPONENTS
(SIMPLIFIED)

IN

IN

WASTE OUT

HOLDING
TANK

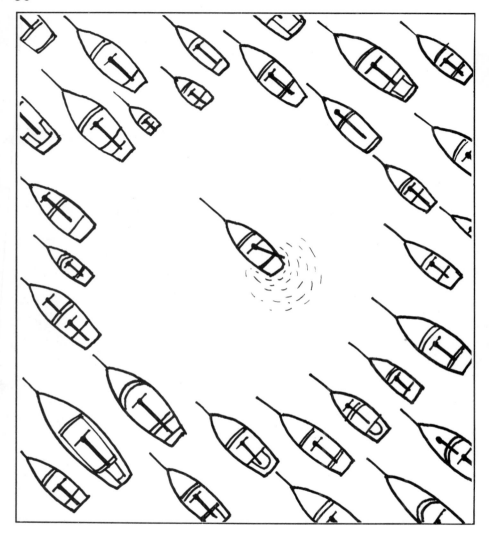

O.K., O.K., This time I'LL hold the valve open and YOU pump.

Head problems, relatively uncommon, are generally easy to correct.

Heading out for a Year in Paradise

Departure
Sept.
12/93

Back
Home
Sept.
10/94

It's been a Great Trip...

Welcome Aboard

MATES	VESSEL	DATE

Welcome Aboard

MATES	VESSEL	DATE